Searchlight
BOOKS™

High-Tech Science

Explore

Drones

Abbe Lynn Starr

Lerner Publications ◆ Minneapolis

Lerner Publications Company
An imprint of Lerner Publishing Group, Inc.
241 First Avenue North
Minneapolis, MN 55401 USA

For reading levels and more information, look up this title
at www.lernerbooks.com.

Main body text set in Adrianna Regular.
Typeface provided by Chank.

Editor: Brianna Kaiser

Library of Congress Cataloging-in-Publication Data

Names: Starr, Abbe L., author.
Title: Explore drones / Abbe Lynn Starr.
Description: Minneapolis : Lerner Publications, [2024] | Series: Searchlight books. High-tech science | Includes bibliographical references and index. | Audience: Ages 8–11 | Audience: Grades 4–6 | Summary: "Drones are commonly used by the military, scientists, and more. Discover the beginning of drones, how and why people use drones today, and where the future of drones could be headed"— Provided by publisher.
Identifiers: LCCN 2023006976 (print) | LCCN 2023006977 (ebook) | ISBN 9798765608937 (lib. bdg.) | ISBN 9798765617021 (epub)
Subjects: LCSH: Drone aircraft—Juvenile literature. | BISAC: JUVENILE NONFICTION / Technology / Robotics
Classification: LCC TL685.35 .S73 2024 (print) | LCC TL685.35 (ebook) | DDC 629.133/39—dc23/eng/20230221

LC record available at https://lccn.loc.gov/2023006976
LC ebook record available at https://lccn.loc.gov/2023006977

Manufactured in the United States of America
1-1009440-51571-4/20/2023

Table of Contents

Chapter 1

HISTORY OF DRONES

There's something in the sky. It looks like an airplane, but wait . . . it's too small to be a plane and it's carrying a package. It's a drone!

Drones are uncrewed flying robots. That means there are no people in the drone. People on the ground control drones with a remote. Some drones have an onboard computer that allows them to fly on their own to a specific location.

Militaries and Uncrewed Aircraft

On June 4, 1783, a crowd of people in Annonay, France, watched an uncrewed hot-air balloon take flight. The Montgolfier brothers, Joseph-Michel and Jacques-Étienne, invented the hot-air balloon. Their invention helped start the use of uncrewed aircraft.

A late 1700s engraving showing the hot-air balloon designed by the Montgolfier brothers

Nikola Tesla experimented with energy and invented radio-controlled technology.

Militaries around the world began using uncrewed aircraft in the 1800s. In 1849, Austria used uncrewed balloon bombs to attack Venice, Italy. The balloon bombs were not very accurate at hitting their target. In 1896, camera technology was added to rockets. This improved the accuracy of uncrewed aircraft.

Two years later, engineer Nikola Tesla invented radio-controlled technology. People in the military looked to see how this could be helpful in war.

Science Fact or Science Fiction?

People thought Nikola Tesla was a magician.

That's a fact! In front of a New York crowd in 1898, Tesla steered a small boat using a remote control. But nothing was connecting the boat to his controller, so the crowd thought he was a magician. Tesla controlled his boat with radio waves—electromagnetic waves used for communication. Tesla's radio-controlled technology was later added to airplanes.

In 1916, British engineer Archibald Low used Tesla's technology to create the Ruston Proctor Aerial Target. This uncrewed plane was controlled with radio guidance. A year later, Low made the first rocket that used radio control.

In 1935, actor Reginald Denny developed a radio-controlled plane for the US military. The US military used uncrewed planes during World War II (1939–1945). In 1939, the US Army Air Corps used Denny's radio-controlled target drone, the Radioplane OQ-2.

A Radioplane OQ-2 target drone

Hurricanes are storms with heavy rains and strong winds.

New Uses

In the 1970s, the US Department of Defense decided to use satellites for a new navigation system. The Global Positioning System (GPS) had many uses such as helping control uncrewed missiles and rockets from around the world.

In the beginning of the 2000s, people found another purpose for drones: search and rescue. Hurricane Katrina hit the southeastern US in August 2005. Strong winds and rains destroyed homes and flooded many areas, especially New Orleans, Louisiana.

Search and rescue teams used drones to fly over flooded neighborhoods and roads that the teams couldn't reach. The drones took video of the damage and sent the information back to the teams. The teams were able to see which areas were most damaged and where people needed help.

Drones can help in search and rescue missions after natural disasters such as Hurricane Katrina.

STEM Spotlight

The US Navy first experimented with satellite navigation in the 1960s to track military submarines. There were six GPS satellites in space. Scientists tracked these satellites and their shifts with radio signals. Then they could see exactly where the submarines were. This is called the Doppler effect. GPS now uses thirty-one satellites. Many people and organizations, including the military, use GPS.

Chapter 2

SHAPES, SIZES, AND SKILLS

Drones are made in many shapes and sizes. That allows them to do different things. A quadcopter is a drone that lifts off the ground with four propellers. This style of aircraft is often used for drones.

Largest and Smallest

Ravn X is one of the largest drones in the world. It has a 60-foot (18 m) wingspan and weighs 55,000 pounds (24,948 kg). It shoots satellites into low Earth orbit. When

A QUADCOPTER WITH A CAMERA ATTACHED TO IT

▼

it lands, Ravn X can park itself into a hangar.

One of the smallest drones in the world is Piccolissimo. The size of a quarter, it has a body and a propeller. The motor spins the body in one direction, while a propeller spins in the other direction. Changing the speed of the propeller causes the drone to change direction.

The DJI Mavic 3 flies over Colorado in 2021.

High and Fast

Drones can fly fast and at amazing heights. The DJI Mavic 3 can fly as high as 30,292 feet (9,233 m). It could fly over Mount Everest! At these heights, the air is thin, cold, and windy. This drone is designed to spin its propellers faster than other drones This prevents getting ice on its blades and allows it to fly in very strong winds.

A drone's speed depends on its shape, size, and weight. Most drones fly 40 to 60 miles (64 to 97 km) per hour. Some people race drones. The world's fastest racing drone can fly about 164 miles (263 km) per hour. The Drone Racing League's RacerX holds the title in *Guinness World Records* for the fastest drone in the world.

A drone flies at the 2019 Tech Drone League Race in Turkey.

One of the fastest military drones was the Falcon Hypersonic Technology Vehicle 2 (HTV-2). It flew up to Mach 20, which is twenty times the speed of sound or about 15,000 miles (24,140 km) per hour. It was designed to reach anywhere in the world within one hour.

In 2011, a rocket test-launched this drone. It stayed in the air at speeds of Mach 20 for three minutes. It then crashed into the Pacific Ocean as planned, and scientists recovered it. This flight taught scientists about the effects of heat on drones.

Chapter 3

MANY PURPOSES

People use drones for many reasons. They can gather information, assist people in jobs, and help keep people away from danger.

Emergency Response

Drones can deliver food and emergency supplies if roads are blocked. Drones help in search and rescue after natural disasters such as earthquakes and fires.

FIREFIGHTERS CAN USE DRONES DURING SEARCH AND RESCUE.

Firefighters rely on information gathered from drones to see where a fire is spreading. This helps firefighters know where to put out fires.

Rescuers use smaller drones when trying to reach those who may be caught in rubble from earthquakes. With heat sensors, drones can send rescuers information on where people are trapped. Drones can send pictures to rescuers of areas where it may be unsafe for them to go. Rescuers then plan how to move over unstable ground and bring help to those who are trapped.

Drones also watch traffic and report when there is an accident. This can help emergency services arrive at the scene as soon as possible. Drones take pictures of new construction and find weak buildings and bridges that need to be repaired. The information helps engineers know where to fix problems.

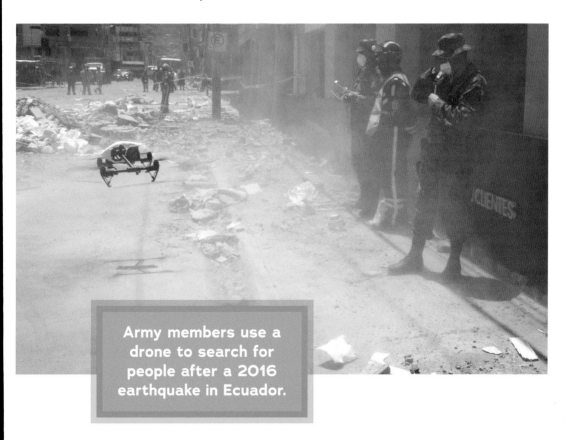

Army members use a drone to search for people after a 2016 earthquake in Ecuador.

Climate Change Activity

With drones, scientists monitor climate change activity. They can gather data about the wildlife patterns of many animals such as penguins in Antarctica and polar bears in the Arctic. Drones can also track dangerous natural events such as strong thunderstorms and wildfires. Then scientists can warn people of the events.

Drones can monitor events such as wildfires.

A DRONE LIFTING A PACKAGE IN A WAREHOUSE

▼

Helping with Jobs

Many businesses use drones to do difficult tasks. In warehouses, drones count the number of items that are stored. Climbing ladders to reach high shelves can be dangerous for people. Drones can reach those products instead, making the job safer for workers.

Drones help farmers take care of their crops. Drones monitor crops and soil health and determine if the crops are too dry or too wet. Drones also spot if insects are eating the crops. Drones spray fertilizers and even plant seeds.

Farmers can use drones to keep an eye on their crops.

Movies and More

Movies use drones to tell a better story. The ability for a drone to move quickly, make difficult turns, and get into small spaces has created film that otherwise would be impossible to shoot. Before movies shoot in a new place, drones can go there and give directors information that will help them prepare.

Drones are also just used for fun! Drone shows are used to celebrate special occasions. At Queen Elizabeth II's 2022 Platinum Jubilee, which honored her seventieth year of reign, drones flew in England in special patterns and colors to create pictures in the sky.

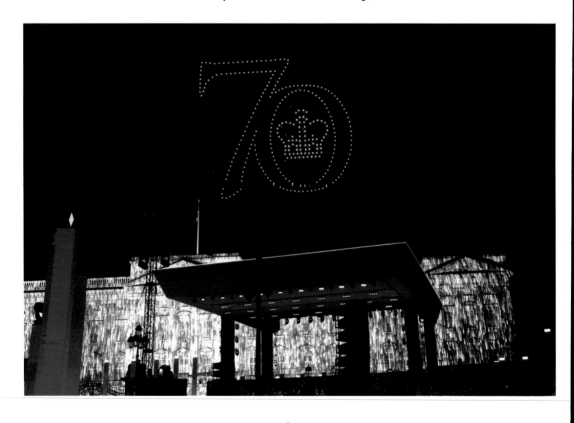

A DRONE SHOW AT QUEEN ELIZABETH II'S 2022 PLATINUM JUBLIEE

Chapter 4

FLYING IN
THE FUTURE

Engineers continue to make drones stronger and faster so they can do more to make people's lives easier. There will always be a place for drones in militaries. The Lockheed Martin SR-72 is a supersonic jet that will be used as a spy tool. Drones such as the SR-72 will gather valuable information and keep military members away from danger.

Deliveries

Drone package deliveries are becoming more common. People may order something online, and a drone will deliver it.

Some quadcopters are being built with legs and talons. These birdlike drones can perch on tree limbs and telephone poles. Flying takes up a lot of energy, so this rest helps the drones save energy. They can also grasp packages with their talons.

The Lockeed Martin SR-71, an earlier model of the SR-72, in flight

Science Fact or Science Fiction?

Drones will pollinate plants.

That's a fact! Over two-thirds of the crops that feed the world rely on bees and other insects to pollinate plants. Because bee populations are declining, fewer plants will be pollinated. Scientist Yiannis Aloimonos is developing a RoboBeeHive. This beehive releases a swarm of miniature bee drones into a field. These tiny drones have furlike legs that will take pollen from plant to plant, similar to what bees do.

The medical world could use drones more often to deliver supplies to places that are difficult to reach or where people are not close to a hospital. Drones will also carry tests from patients to labs that require a fast delivery. A careful, quick organ donation delivery could save someone's life.

The company Zipline delivers medical supplies to people who don't live near hospitals.

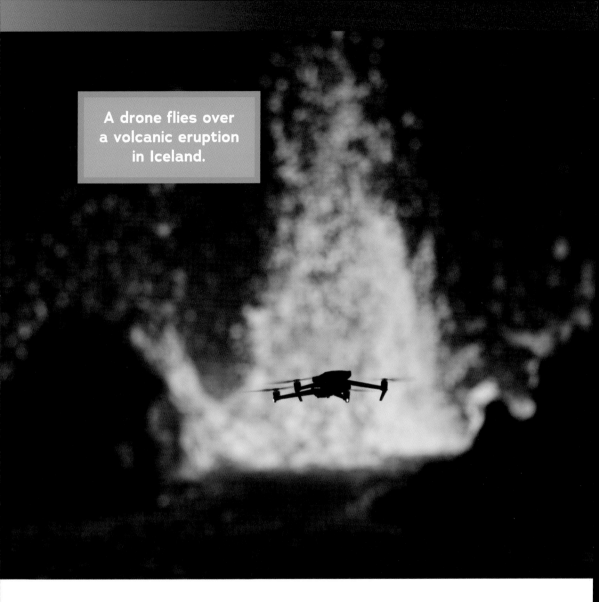

A drone flies over a volcanic eruption in Iceland.

Helpful Tech

It is likely that you have seen drones in your city or neighborhood. With so many ways to use drones, they will become more common. This technology serves people now and will be helpful in the future. What will drones do next?

Glossary

accurate: correct in action

electromagnetic: an interaction that occurs between atoms and molecules with an electric charge

guidance: directing the motion or position of something

missile: a weapon that propels itself to its target before exploding

monitor: to watch or keep track of

navigation: the act of finding a correct path through an area

pollinate: to transfer pollen to a plant to allow it to fertilize

propeller: blades that spin to make an aircraft move

search and rescue: an operation where trained emergency workers find and rescue people

uncrewed aircraft: something that flies without a person on board

Learn More

Academic Kids: Unmanned Aerial Vehicle
https://academickids.com/encyclopedia/index.php/UAV

Brainard, Jason. *Drones for Fun*. New York: PowerKids, 2020.

Britannica Kids: Drones
https://kids.britannica.com/kids/assembly/view/214255

Conley, Kate. *Inside Drones*. Minneapolis: Core Library, 2019.

Kiddle: Unmanned Aerial Vehicle Facts for Kids
https://kids.kiddle.co/Unmanned_aerial_vehicle

Starr, Abbe Lynn. *Explore Robotics*. Minneapolis: Lerner Publications, 2024.

Index

Photo Acknowledgments

Image credits: Universal History Archive/Universal Images/Getty Images, p. 5; Mondadori Portfolio/Mondadori/Getty Images, p. 6; Eraza Collection/Alamy, p. 8; donald_gruener/Getty Images, p. 9; Warren Faidley/Getty Images, p. 10; Kypros/Getty Images, p. 13; marekuliasz/Shutterstock, pp. 14–15; Muhammed Enes Yildirim/Anadolu Agency/Getty Images, p. 16; Sobrevolando Patagonia/Shutterstock, p. 18; Fotos593/Shutterstock, p. 19; Patrick Orton/Getty Images, p. 20; Vithun Khamsong/Getty Images, p. 21; baranozdemir/Getty Images, pp. 22–23; Chris Jackson/Getty Images, p. 24; guvendemir/Getty Images, p. 26; Joerg Boethling/Alamy, p. 28; Abstract Aerial Art/Getty Images, p. 29.

Cover: PA Images/Alamy Stock Photo.